Tracing Our JEWISH Roots

MIRIAM SAGAN

John Muir Publications
Santa Fe, New Mexico

Acknowledgments
Many thanks to Jan Best, Kath Lee, Sarah Lovett, Russell Smith, and Robert Winson for support and help with this book.

Dedicated to my grandparents, George and Esther Sagan, Sadie and Avrum Giller
        To my parents, Frimi Giller Sagan and Eli Sagan
        To my daughter, Isabel Winson-Sagan

John Muir Publications, P.O. Box 613, Santa Fe, New Mexico 87504
© 1993 by John Muir Publications
All rights reserved. Published 1993
Printed in the United States of America
Printed on recycled paper

First edition. First printing October 1993
        First TWG printing October 1993

Library of Congress Cataloging-in-Publication Data
Sagan, Miriam, 1954-
American origins : tracing our Jewish roots / by Miriam Sagan.
        p.   cm.
   Includes index.
   Summary: Traces the history of Jews, especially those from Eastern Europe, in the United States, their experiences as immigrants, and their contributions to American culture.
ISBN 1-56261-151-8 : $12.95
1. Jews—United States—History—Juvenile literature. 2. Jews, East European—United States—History—Juvenile literature. 3. Jews—Europe, Eastern—History—Juvenile literature. 4. Immigrants—United States—History—Juvenile literature. 5. United States—Ethnic relations—Juvenile literature. 6. Europe, Eastern—Ethnic relations—Juvenile literature. [1. Jews—United States—History. 2. Jews, East European. 3. United States—Emigration and immigration.]
I. Title.
E184.J5S24 1993
973'.04924—dc20   93-14596
                                                                CIP
                                                                AC

Logo design: Peter Aschwanden
Interior design: Ken Wilson
Illustrations: Beth Evans
Typography: Ken Wilson
Printer: Guynes Printing Company
Bindery: Prizma Industries, Inc.

Distributed to the book trade by
W. W. Norton & Co., Inc.
500 Fifth Avenue
New York, New York 10110

Distributed to the education market by
The Wright Group
19201 120th Avenue N.E.
Bothell, WA 98011-9512

Cover photo, Jewish life in Biala, Poland, The Bettmann Archive
Title page photo, immigrants arriving in America, The Bettmann Archive
Back cover photo, boys pitching pennies in New York City, New York Public Library

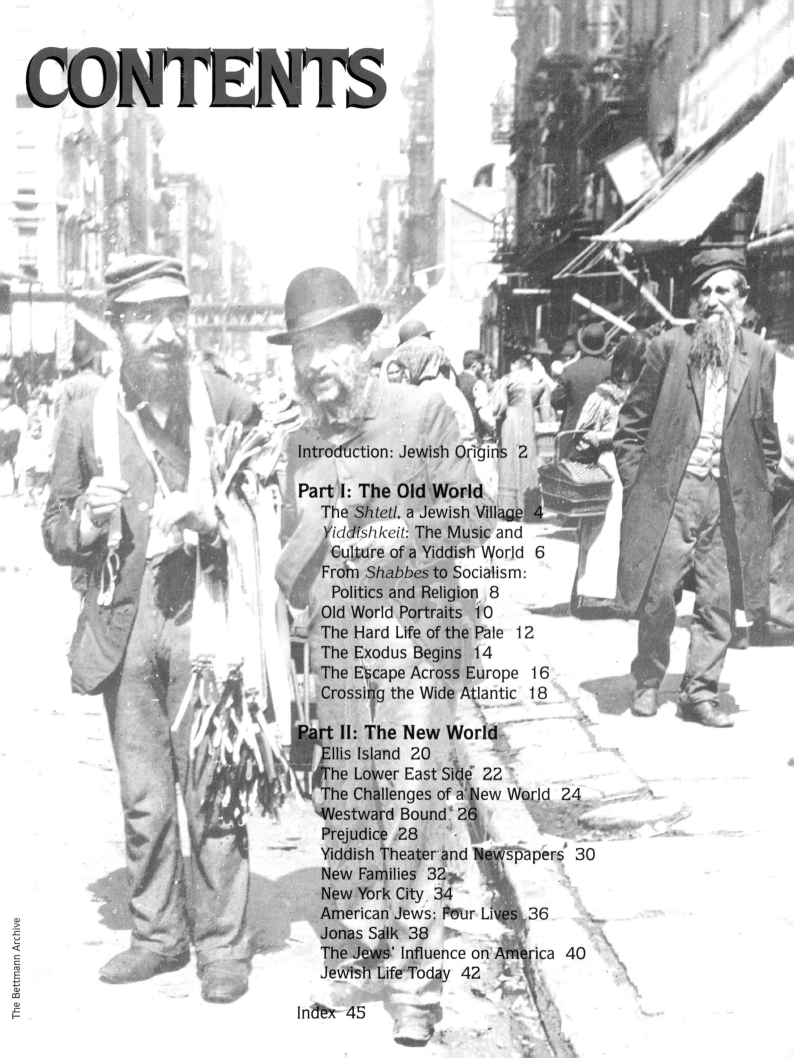

CONTENTS

JEWISH ORIGINS

Who are the Jewish people? They speak many languages and come from many countries. Some are religious, and some are not. But what all Jewish people have in common is a shared history.

Early Jewish history is recorded in the Old Testament. There, Moses leads the Jews out of slavery in Egypt to the promised land of Palestine. Later, King David, one of the Jews' early kings, defeated the Jews' enemies and brought his people peace and prosperity in Palestine for many years. More than 2,000 years ago, the Romans conquered the Jews and destroyed their holy city, Jerusalem. And after the Roman Empire collapsed, most of the Jews were forced out of Palestine, many fleeing into Europe. This scattering of the Jews out of Palestine is known as the diaspora.

Sometimes the Jews in Europe were allowed to live in peace. Other times were full of trouble for them. In 1492, the same year Columbus landed in the Americas, all Jews were expelled from Spain. Many had lived there for centuries in safe communities. Many of these Spanish Jews fled east into Europe, particularly into Russia, Poland, and Germany.

Some of the Spanish Jews pretended to convert to Christianity and stayed in Spain. Some of these Jews traveled with the Spanish explorers and conquerors to South and Central America in the 1500s. These were the first Jews to come to the New World.

The Bettmann Archive

Peasant life in Russia

How Many Jews Came to America?

Decade	Number
1790-1880	180,000
1881-1890	200,000
1891-1900	300,000
1901-1910	1,074,442
1911-1920	152,000
1921-1930	130,000
1931-1975	570,000

Between 1882 and 1924, 1.8 million Jews entered the United States. In 1924, the Jewish population in America was 4.2 million. Restrictive immigration laws and the Great Depression lowered the number of Jews coming to America in the 1920s and 1930s. Immigration picked up before and after WWII. Today, most of the world's 17.5 million Jews live in Israel, the United States, Europe, and the former Soviet Union.

Jews came to America from all parts of Europe, including an area called "the Pale." The names and boundaries of many European countries have changed over the years.

The first Jews to arrive in New York City, then called New Amsterdam, were 23 people fleeing from religious persecution in Brazil in 1654. They had pretended to be Christians, but the Brazilians discovered they were Jews and drove them out of Brazil. Over the years that followed, small numbers of other Jews found their way to the American colonies. The first Jewish synagogue in America was built in Rhode Island in 1763.

During the American Revolution, most American Jews joined in the rebellion against the British. Francis Salvador was the first Jew to die in battle, in 1776. Another Jewish soldier, Abraham Solomon, fought in the Battle of Bunker Hill. And the Jewish community was a strong supporter of the new Constitution written in 1789.

Who were these Jews in the new United States? They were hatters and shoemakers, silversmiths and coppersmiths, butchers, watchmakers, shopkeepers, embroiderers, printers, innkeepers, tailors, and chocolate-makers.

For the Jews of Europe in the 1800s, whose lives were hard, America was a golden land to dream about. Many Jews left Germany for the United States during the first wave of immigration, from about 1830 to 1880. Even more Jews came from Russia and Poland during the second wave of immigration, from 1881 to 1924. The majority of Jewish families in America today can trace their roots back to these Jews from small villages in Europe, who left behind a life of fear and poverty.

The United States welcomed Jewish immigrants and gave them freedom. It also presented them with new problems and challenges.

3

THE *SHTETL,* A JEWISH VILLAGE

The Jews of eastern Europe shared a history and a way of life. Most important, they shared the language of Yiddish. Hebrew is the holy language of the Jews, while Yiddish is the lively language of daily life. An important word in Yiddish is *shtetl, (SHTEH-t'l)* which means "little town" or "village."

The shtetls of eastern Europe were very poor but spirited. Typically, they were crowded villages with cobblestones, alleys, narrow lanes, and ragged wooden houses. A market, where merchants sold everything from garlic to fish, was open on all but the coldest days. Because Jews were very restricted by prejudice, many occupations and opportunities were closed to them. For example, by law, Jews could not own property, so the shtetl folk worked mostly in humble professions as butchers, bakers, cobblers, and seamstresses.

What did kids do in the shtetl? Study, study, and study. They studied religion, Hebrew, the Bible, and Jewish law. They studied together from dawn to dusk, six days a week, in a special building or room called a *heder* (school). Jewish boys began studying as early as age three and would certainly be disgraced if they could not read Hebrew by the time they were six. On the first day of school, a boy's mother would feed him a little honey cake for each letter of the alphabet, so that he would come to think of learning as sweet.

The Bettmann Archive

Baking matzoh, an unleavened bread, for the Passover holiday

Yiddish takes words from German, Hebrew, Polish, and even English. Some useful words in Yiddish are:

mazel tov! (MAH-zehl tohv), **congratulations**

maven (MAY-ven), **an expert**

schnorrer (SHNOHR-er), **a bum, someone who whines and begs, a cheapskate**

plotz (plots), **to explode, to burst, either from happiness or misery**

shlemiel (shleh-MEEL), **a fool or an idiot**

sholem (SHAH-lem), **Yiddish pronunciation of the Hebrew** *shalom,* **which means peace**

Neighbors in the shtetl

Jewish religious law governed every aspect of daily life. If a cow wandered into a neighbor's pasture and the two neighbors quarreled, a rabbi, or learned teacher, would be called in to settle the dispute. Laws and rituals also governed the preparation of food. Food eaten in the shtetl had to be kosher, or fit to eat according to Jewish law. One of the main rules, then and now, prohibits eating meat and dairy products at the same time. (A cheese-burger, for example, is definitely not kosher.)

Eastern European Jewish cooking, which was always kosher, produced many delicious recipes. Often the mother of a family had to cook with few or poor ingredients, but she prided herself on serving delicious and filling meals. She might serve blintzes, a pan-cake rolled around a filling such as cottage cheese or jam, and covered in sour cream. Or she might prepare borscht, a beet soup that became a common meal because beets were inexpensive. Bialies, excellent rolls often sprinkled with onions, took their name from Bialystok, a city in Poland. The bagel, a hard, doughnut-shaped roll made from white flour, was a delicacy in the shtetl.

The Jewish families of the shtetl depended on each other. The job of men and boys was to study and be religious; the job of women and girls, to keep the household, cook, and sometimes even support the family.

Most Jewish boys could read Hebrew by the time they were six

YIDDISHKEIT: THE OF A YIDDISH WORLD

The life of European Jewish villagers was a hard one. They were poor and often suffered from persecution. But the folk culture of the villagers helped them keep their spirits up despite their troubles. This culture was called *Yiddishkeit (yid-dish-KITE)*, from Yiddish, the language that eastern European Jews shared no matter what country they lived in.

In the shtetl there were no televisions, no movies, no telephones, and very little opportunity for travel. So traveling musicians were greeted with great excitement. These ragged players were called klezmer musicians, and they played their haunting melodies on everything from cellos and drums to violins and clarinets. Although most klezmer musicians could not read music, they played wedding songs, hymns, and wild gypsy tunes that drew even the oldest grandmother and the youngest toddler into the dance.

Among religious Jews, there were strict rules of behavior. Men and women were not allowed to touch each other when they danced. Certainly a dance like the waltz was impossible, and so men and women often danced in separate groups. When a man and a woman did dance together, rather than hold hands they grasped the corners of a handkerchief held between them. At weddings, klezmer musicians played special songs for leading the bride to her seat and then toe-tapping tunes for dancing in a line. Wedding guests lifted the bride and groom in their chairs high above the dancing crowd to honor them as king and queen of the day.

The painter Marc Chagall took with him these images of eastern Europe when he went to paint in Paris. In his paintings, the bride and groom seem to fly through the air as they dance. One of his most famous works

A bride and groom under the traditional canopy

A favorite Jewish story involves a woman who lives with a large family crowded into one room. She goes to the rabbi to ask for help. He suggests that she move in first her chickens, then her goats, and finally her cow. The single room is now completely crowded. "What should I do?" she asks. "Take out the cow," the rabbi suggests. The next day she thanks him, for the room really seems bigger without the cow! What moral do you think villagers might have taken from this story?

MUSIC AND CULT

The Bettmann Archive

Klezmer music is still popular today

shows a klezmer musician, violin in hand, standing on a rooftop. This image of shtetl life represents the villagers' ability to enjoy life even under difficult circumstances.

Around a fire at night, or seated with quilts on the ledges of a Russian-style stove, children listened to their grandparents tell stories. They heard stories of Bible figures and of ghosts and demons. Jokes and riddles added fun to long winter evenings when the world was covered in snow and quiet. Sometimes the talk turned to that golden land, America.

Some young men left the village to go to bigger cities such as Warsaw. There, they might work in a shop for 14 hours a day and still talk about art and politics far into the night. Believers in Yiddishkeit, these young writers and poets talked together in Yiddish about the hardships in their lives. But they

also talked about their hopes for a better life, which burned inside them with a small but sure flame.

Storytelling on a cold winter's night

ROM *SHABBES* TO AND RELIGION

Imagine if instead of celebrating just a few holidays a year, you celebrated one every week. For the Jews of eastern Europe, the Sabbath was a true holiday. Called *shabbes (SHAH-bes)* in Yiddish, the day of rest began at sunset on Friday night and ended Saturday evening when three stars had appeared in the sky. Shabbes was called "The Queen of the Week," and it was a day of celebration in a hard life. Shabbes began with the mother of the house lighting a pair of candles and making a blessing over a cup of wine and braided loaves of bread called *challah (KHAH-lah)*. Dinner was a feast, with a chicken dish if the family could afford it. If you were a stranger or a traveler, a poor person or a lonely student, you could always count on a family to invite you to join them in the celebration of shabbes.

Religious people wore dark, modest clothing. Men wore a prayer shawl with fringes, called a *tallis (TAL-us)*, and on their heads a skullcap, called a *yarmulke (YAHR-m'l-kuh)*. Even the smallest boys wore these. Women covered their heads after they were married, with scarves or wigs, to show they were modest. The leaders of the religious community were the rabbis, spiritual teachers who explained Jewish religious law.

The difficult life of the Jews made many of them search for something better. Some joined Hasidism, a strong, strict religious movement. The Hasidim (KHAH-sid-im), which means "the pious" in Hebrew, felt that God could be worshiped anywhere, even in a field. Hasids sang and danced as they prayed, and they attracted many joyful followers.

No shabbes dinner was complete without chicken soup. And chicken soup needs noodles. Here's how to make those noodles:

Beat two eggs with a bit of pepper and salt. Add flour until it is a stiff paste. Flour a cutting board, and then roll out the paste until it is very, very thin. Let it dry for two hours. Now cut the dough into strips about 3 inches long by 1 inch wide. Stack them and cut again into matchlike strips. Separate them by tossing, and spread them out to dry. Then toss them into boiling chicken soup and boil for ten minutes. Delicious!

s dress includes the prayer shawl,
allis

SOCIALISM: POLITICS

Joyful Hasids dance to worship God

For other Jews in eastern Europe, politics was the answer. Many Jews became followers of socialism. They believed that all people are equal and should have control over their work and the goods they produce. Some Jews also believed that the Jewish people deserved their own homeland, and they longed to return to the land of Israel. This political and spiritual movement was called Zionism. Hasidism, socialism, and Zionism all stirred the desire for change among the European Jews. Onto this rich soil fell the seeds of a new idea: immigration to the United States. For many, the idea of moving to America, the land of freedom, became a burning desire.

Shabbes did not stay in the Old World when the Jews left for the friendlier shores of America. "The Queen of the Week" came with her people, even to the noisy slums of New York. There, amid the bustle of a new world, Jews celebrated the Sabbath as a time to be together and honor their families and community.

The elders of a proud Jewish family

OLD WORLD PORTRAITS

Many European Jews were creative and studious. They excelled as writers and intellectuals. Jewish education focused on learning to think clearly and to debate ideas. This led many Jews into interesting—and sometimes totally new—ways of thinking.

Sholom Aleichem (1859–1916)

Sholom Aleichem was an important writer in Yiddish. Sholom Aleichem was not his real name, of course: it means "peace be with you." He was born Sholem or Solomon Rabinowitz. Why do you think he took this pen name? Maybe he wanted to tell his readers that his work would be funny and full of love. It was. One of his favorite characters was Tevye, the dairyman who always told a

Sholom Aleichem, "the Yiddish Mark Twain"

joke no matter what his troubles. Sholom Aleichem was born in the Ukraine in Russia. In 1906, he immigrated to New York City, where he spent the rest of his life. Many of his readers were also immigrants. Because of his humor and sharp wit, Sholom Aleichem is called "the Yiddish Mark Twain" after the humorous American novelist.

Leon Trotsky (1879–1940)

Another Russian Jew, Leon Trotsky also wrote—but not to entertain. He was a radical socialist who plotted to overthrow the tsar, the ruler of Russia. Trotsky's real name was Lev Davidovich Bronstein, and he was born into a comfortable family. Because of his politics, he was exiled to Siberia. Later, he helped organize the uprising—the Bolshevik Revolution of 1917—that overthrew the tsar. But revolutionaries do not always agree with each other, and Trotsky was expelled from Russia in 1929. Even leaving the country did not put an end to his problems. He was murdered in Mexico in 1940, most likely by followers of Stalin, his rival for power.

Leon Trotsky, a leader of the Bolshevik Revolution

Sigmund Freud (1856–1939)

Not all thinkers who work for change need to overthrow governments. Sigmund Freud changed the way we think by looking inside himself and others. Freud was a doctor in Vienna, Austria, and one of the founding fathers of psychology. Psychology is the study of how human beings behave and feel. During Freud's day, many people thought that children were not very important and that their feelings didn't count. But Freud thought that what happens to us during childhood shapes our whole lives. He encouraged his patients to talk about their dreams and childhood memories to relieve their sadness, guilt, or other troubling feelings. This method is called psychoanalysis and is widely used today. In 1938 Freud was forced to flee from the Nazis and lived the rest of his life in London, writing and teaching.

I. B. Singer (left) receiving his Nobel Prize

Sigmund Freud, the father of psychoanalysis

Isaac Bashevis Singer (1904–1991)

The writer Isaac Bashevis Singer drew on his childhood memories to write many of his stories. Born in Poland, he was influenced by Sholom Aleichem and also wrote in Yiddish.

You have probably never read anything in Yiddish. Indeed, most Jewish people in America can no longer read it. Why did a popular writer like Isaac Bashevis Singer continue to write in this language? When a reporter asked him this question, he laughed and said, "On the Day of Judgment, when all the old Jews come back to life, they'll want to know what is new in the world. And I wrote my stories in Yiddish for them!"

His stories and novels are full of adventure—of devils and fools, ghosts and beauties, magicians and acrobats. His books for children include *Zlateh the Goat* and *Mazel and Schlimazel*, an amusing tale about a battle between the spirit of bad luck and the spirit of good luck. I. B. Singer won the Nobel Prize, the highest honor in literature, and lived the rest of his years in Florida.

THE HARD LIFE OF THE PALE

Because of prejudice against Jews, Jews in Russia were allowed to live only within a certain area called "the Pale of Settlement." This area covered 386,000 square miles and extended from the Baltic to the Black Sea. That is more than twice the size of California. It included Galicia, the southern part of Poland. About 95 percent of Polish and Russian Jews lived within the Pale; only a lucky few were granted permission to live outside. Even within the Pale, Jews were restricted to certain towns and cities.

The Russian rulers, called tsars, did not allow anyone to vote, and they did not believe in religious freedom. They tried to force the Jews to become Christians. Also, many people were anti-Semitic, meaning that they hated Jews simply for being Jewish. As a result, the Jews of the Pale were frequently victims of *pogroms (POH-grums)*, which are massacres or violent persecutions. Horsemen would ride into Jewish villages and destroy them, burning houses and killing people.

Anti-Semitism is hatred of Jews simply because they are Jewish. Sometimes anti-Semitism in the Pale took the form of unfair laws that discriminated against Jews, and sometimes it took the form of actual hostility and violence, even by neighbors. Throughout history, prejudice forced Jews to flee from country to country. In the twentieth century, the anti-Semitism of Adolf Hitler, the leader of Nazi Germany (1933–1945), led him to order the murder of six million Jews, many in concentration camps. Many Jews and non-Jews alike hope that the world's remembrance of this event will prevent future Holocausts. Their rallying cry is, "Never again."

During a pogrom, people fled for their lives

The tsars encouraged these pogroms against the Jews.

Under the reign of Nicholas I, the tsar of Russia from 1825 to 1855, things got worse for the Jews of the Pale. During that period, 600 anti-Jewish laws were enacted. Tsar Nicholas wanted to destroy the Jewish community, religion, and way of life. Most dreadful of these laws was one that required Jewish boys to join the army. Being drafted into the Russian army was a terrible fate.

Imagine that one day when you are 12 years old, a group of soldiers comes through your town. You might be sitting at your desk or playing outside your house. Suddenly one of the soldiers grabs you and takes you from your family, home, friends, and everything that is familiar. You barely have a chance to pack or say good-bye. In the army, you walk for ten hours a day in the mud. You are given only a biscuit to eat, and you receive sneers and beatings from the officers. Worst of all, you must stay in the army for 25 years. Soldiers sometimes took boys as young as eight or nine, who often died on the long, terrible marches. When families saw the tsar's soldiers coming, they hid their children. Sometimes they even cut off a son's finger or toe so that he would be considered unfit for the army.

In the Pale, the Jews feared everything: the tsar, the government, the army, and the law. For them, the Pale would always be a land of trouble and danger.

Tsar Nicholas I

THE EXODUS BEGINS

Between 1826 and 1850, about 45,000 Jews left Europe bound for the United States. Most of them were from Germany, Austria, and Hungary. These immigrants were usually called German Jews, even though not all were actually from Germany.

German Jews were less traditional than eastern European Jews. Most went to non-religious schools as children and practiced a form of Judaism that was more modern than that practiced by the Russian Jews. They suffered from prejudice because they were Jews, but they were more integrated into society than the eastern European Jews, who had been restricted to cities and shtetls in the Pale.

Why did the German Jews leave Europe? They were part of the large early wave of German immigration to America. Along with their countrymen, German Jews were eager to escape poverty and political repression. Revolutions swept through Europe in the mid-1800s but failed to improve their lives. Many German Jews began to believe their chance for progress and freedom lay across the ocean.

Eastern European Jews had other reasons for leaving Europe. Most Jews of the shtetls continued to suffer from heavy taxes and restrictions on their right to marry, find work, and set up households. In Russia, conditions for Jews worsened toward the end of the nineteenth century. When the open-minded Tsar Alexander II was assassinated in 1881, the event set off a new series of attacks on Russian Jews. The new regime encouraged pogroms against Jewish communities, and many Jews were thrown out of their villages. In 1891, 20,000 Jews were told they could no longer live in Moscow. In 1905, the

The Bettmann Archive

Jewish refugees leaving Russia

Goldeneh medina **meant "golden country," but it had another meaning as well—"fool's paradise," a false gold that shone brightly but was worthless. The Jews knew that America might present new struggles they could only imagine. In some traditional Jewish communities, a person who had gone to America was considered to be dead. People wept when they saw the emigrant off at the station and prayed for him afterward. Many believed that America was an unholy place, where no one observed the Sabbath, where tradition was forgotten, and where Jews lost their identity. Only time would tell if America was truly a golden country, or simply a fool's paradise.**

Waiting to set sail for the U.S.

government crushed a growing movement for Jewish freedom. More and more Jews came to believe there was only one solution to their problems—an exodus to America.

What did America mean to the Jews of eastern Europe? They called it the *goldeneh medina (GOLD-en-eh meh-DEE-neh)*, the "golden country," where the streets were paved with gold. Of course, no one thought that the streets actually had cobblestones of the yellow metal. Instead, it was an expression of optimism and hope. America became a symbol of freedom and justice. It meant no more pogroms in which Jews died or watched their houses burn. It meant no more young boys snatched from their families to serve in a cruel army. It meant the chance to pursue their dreams free from discrimination.

Eventually, one-third of all Jews living in eastern Europe left, the majority of them bound for America. Often, the father of a family went first to the New World to see if he could make his way, then sent for his family later. The shtetls of eastern Europe began to empty out as fathers, then whole families, and then even grandparents decided to take a chance on a new life that surely would be better than the one at home.

Leaving the Old Country

THE ESCAPE ACROSS EUROPE

If you want to travel somewhere in the United States, you don't need permission from the government to make the trip. You simply decide if you can afford to travel and whether to go by train, airplane, or car. You do not need a passport to go from New Jersey to Nebraska, and with a passport, you can travel freely to most parts of the world outside the United States.

For the Jews who wanted to leave eastern Europe, the decision was not nearly so simple. Jews were not allowed to travel freely. Remember, they were required to live only in certain cities and villages within the Pale. To get to America they first had to cross secretly from southern Russia into Austria and Hungary.

By 1899, there was a different kind of emigrant, called *fusgeyer (FOOS-gyr)*, which means "walkers" or "wayfarers." The fusgeyer came from Romania, where about one-third of the Jewish population left to come to the United States. These were healthy young men, mostly workers, full of optimism and a thirst for adventure. They banded together and trained themselves to walk long distances because their feet were the only transportation they could afford. They sold what they owned to raise traveling money and took an oath to share everything with each other. These fusgeyer looked like hikers, often wearing khaki clothing and carrying water bottles. They were greeted warmly as they traveled from one Jewish community to another.

Many of the Jews who left did not have legal passports. For them, the first major hurdle was crossing the border into Germany, Austria, or Hungary. Smugglers helped people cross secretly for a price. Sometimes the smugglers would take them part-way and

The author's grandfather, Avrum Giller, as a young man

My maternal grandfather, Avrum Giller, did not intend to leave Russia for good when he took a job building ships in Hamburg, Germany. But when the First World War broke out, it looked like a good time to leave for the United States. His entire savings were a few hundred dollars in gold coins stamped with a picture of the tsar. But after he reached America, he found that his money was worthless. The Bolshevik Revolution had begun in Russia, so no one in America would exchange his old coins for American money. He found work in the Quincy shipyards in Boston, but he never saw his father or mother again.

Fusgeyer, which means "wayfarers," trekked miles across Europe

then refuse to continue until they were paid more money.

Those lucky enough to survive the long and difficult trip across Europe faced another serious problem when they reached the ocean. No traveler with a contagious disease was allowed on a boat. So families were faced with a terrifying dockside inspection for disease. Imagine the despair a mother felt when told her child could not accompany her to America because of an eye infection or tuberculosis. Those who were turned back were left homeless and starving in the port cities of Europe. Add to this the dangers of stolen luggage, receiving tickets to the wrong destination, unfair lodging prices, and a horde of crooks and con men who preyed upon the hapless travelers. The dangers were many—and the journey across the Atlantic had not even begun.

So the Jews left Europe, some walking proudly together and some smuggled out in carts of hay or potatoes. Many grieved for the old homes they would never see again, but most looked forward to a new life in America. In the beginning, a trickle of single men made the almost impossible journey from Europe to America. As conditions for the Jews worsened, this trickle became a flood of hundreds of thousands of Jewish families.

The dockside inspection was a frightening experience

CROSSING THE WIDE ATLANTIC

The trip across the Atlantic Ocean, which could take up to 45 days, was often uncomfortable and unpleasant. It was a farewell to the old life without yet starting the new.

Most immigrants were crowded together under the deck of the ship in an area called steerage. There, they traveled more like baggage than human beings, unlike the wealthier passengers who had comfortable berths above deck. Steerage was dark and dirty. Simple wooden bunks were usually the only furniture. There was often only one washroom for hundreds of people. Ten faucets of cold salt water were all that was provided. The immigrants were often seasick, babies cried endlessly, and the smell of garlic, tobacco, and people was overwhelming.

Fortunately, conditions on the ships did improve by the turn of the century. The German shipping lines offered better steerage accommodations and introduced ships, such as the *Kaiser Wilhelm*, that could make the trip from Hamburg to New York in a record six days.

But the passage to America was not entirely bleak. Young people in particular were happy and excited. There were card games to pass the long hours. Sometimes a musician took his violin out of its old battered case and played a tune, and people danced, forgetting their cares for a while. The more studious passengers pored over their English dictionaries, trying to learn a few phrases of the new language that would be their passport to a better life.

By 1884, at the entrance to New York harbor, stood the welcoming figure of the Statue of Liberty on Liberty Island. At the base of the statue was engraved a poem titled "The New Colossus," written by a German Jew named Emma Lazarus (1849– 1887), which welcomed refugees to the new land. "Give me your tired, your poor, your huddled

Keeping the little ones safe

My paternal grandfather, George Sagan, left Europe when he was a young teenager. In his care were his two nephews and a niece, small children barely able to toddle. Their mother had died in Russia, and he was taking them to New York to meet their father, who had made the voyage earlier. On the journey over, George was constantly worried that the children would get lost or fall overboard. So he tied a rope around the waist of each of the three little ones and kept one hand on that rope during the entire trip.

Immigrant ships were crowded and uncomfortable

masses yearning to breathe free," reads a famous line of the poem. These words came to symbolize America's open door to people emigrating from far-away lands.

But Liberty Island was not the only island in the harbor. There was also Ellis Island, where immigrants learned their fate. Would they be allowed entry to the United States or be turned back? The travelers were flooded with emotion as they came up from steerage to stand on deck for a first glimpse of America. Men in hats and traditional dark clothing stood next to more cheerfully dressed people. Women held babies wrapped in shawls. Butchers, seamstresses, rabbis, and young mothers all wondered how they would be able to work and survive.

Who were these Jews standing on the deck, looking for the first time at America? Unlike some other immigrant groups, the Jewish migration was primarily composed of families. About one-fourth of all Jewish immigrants were children. And a large percentage were young people traveling on their own.

But they all had one thing in common; they all dreamed of beginning their lives anew in America. At last their dream was coming true—for better or worse.

Praying during the long voyage

ELLIS ISLAND

Imagine what it would have been like to arrive as one of these immigrants. You long to set foot on the streets of America. But first you must go through a processing center on an island off the coast of New York. You know that again you must pass a medical examination, and you have heard that you will be asked many questions. You have heard that many people are not allowed to stay in America and must return to Europe. You and your family gather your few belongings and join the crush of fellow immigrants walking down the ship's plank to the doors of Ellis Island. You enter an enormous building with massive halls and dozens of confusing lines. There is a babble of many languages, and you see people of many nationalities. Most con-fusing, the officials are speaking English, a language you do not understand.

For many new arrivals, Ellis Island was a terrifying and confusing stop, the last hurdle to entering America. Some people called it the Day of Judgment. Some people called the building the "Hall of Tears" because of the powerful emotions they felt there. Immigrants were checked for leprosy and tuberculosis and had their eyes examined. All children over the age of two had to show that they could walk by themselves.

Then it was off to another long line, where officials would ask the immigrants questions. Did they have money? Relatives in the United States? A job? Could they read and write? Eastern European Jews were used to dealing with a dishonest government in Europe. There, to get things done, they had been forced to lie and, often, to bribe officials. It was hard for them to believe that the officials at Ellis Island were different and perhaps even had the immigrants' best interests at heart. Immigrants might claim they had a job waiting for them because they thought that's

The Bettmann Archive

Newcomers to America, 1910

One common Ellis Island experience was that an immigrant's name was changed accidentally by immigration officials. Few of these officials understood European languages. My grandfather arrived at Ellis Island as Avrum Guelrud. His last name meant "yellow wheel" in Yiddish, because his father and his father's father had been millers. The official asked him his name and then wrote it on the form as "Giller." So my grandfather left Ellis Island with a new name. It was easier for Americans to spell and pronounce, but he had lost a part of his family history.

Weary immigrants reach American shores at last

what the officials wanted to hear. They did not know that having a pre-arranged job violated American law at the time. Bewildered and confused, immigrants often did not know how to answer the questions put to them.

Fortunately, there were Jewish agencies to help. The Hebrew Immigration Aid Society sent representatives to talk to the new arrivals as they stood in line. These representatives wore caps embroidered with the society's initials, HIAS, so that everyone would know they were there to help.

If no problems arose, it took the average person about a day to pass through Ellis Island. The buildings on the island were overcrowded. During 1907 more than 15,000 immigrants arrived every day, but only 5,000 people could be examined each day. Sometimes people had to wait several days on the ships before entering the processing center. The immigration officials were often overworked, tired, and impatient.

The immigrants stood for hours in long lines that seemed never to move. Some of them pinned doctor's cards to their coats to alert the HIAS that they needed help. All of them worried that they would be sent back to Europe. Fortunately, Jewish self-help and charitable organizations worked overtime to make sure as few immigrants as possible were turned back. Ferries ran 24 hours a day to take those who passed the final test to the streets of New York to begin their new lives.

Ellis Island

THE LOWER EAST SIDE

Manhattan's Lower East Side was the destination for many eastern European Jewish immigrants. Jewish families lived crowded together in run-down, narrow apartment buildings called tenements. A typical family of six lived in only three rooms—and rented part of that space to a boarder. In 1878, there were 300,000 Jews in the United States, and by 1895, there were that number in New York City alone. In 1910, a 1.5-square-mile area of New York's Lower East Side was home to more than half a million Jewish immigrants.

An average block in the Lower East Side had not only overcrowded tenements but

A woman carries a bundle of clothing to be finished at home

synagogues, cafés, theaters, and bars. Because apartments were hot and airless, much of life took place on the bustling streets. Pushcarts sold savory snacks, neighbors gossiped, and children played energetically despite the dangers of traffic.

A bustling street market

The streets of the Lower East Side belonged to the children. Hester Street, Cherry Street, the Bowery—each was an adventure. In the summer heat, children danced under the shower of a water hydrant. Boys played stoopball or stickball. Girls played hopscotch and jacks. Adventurous boys even swam in the murky East River. Children who could not afford a bat played "kick the can." The streets meant work as well as play for children. Girls picked up sewing for their mothers, and boys peddled matches and shined shoes when they were not in school.

Pitching pennies was a favorite pastime

Almost half of the Jews of the Lower East Side worked making clothes in the garment industry. Conditions were terrible. The factories were called "sweatshops" because men and women bent over their sewing machines in hot, poorly lit, badly ventilated rooms. Often women sewed pieces at home, making only a tiny pittance for their hard labor, squeezed in at the end of an already demanding day of housework and caring for children. Wages were very low, even by the standards of the times. In 1914, garment workers earned only 35 cents an hour.

There were other ways to make a living in the new country. Some Jews became milkmen, butchers, grocers, restaurant keepers, booksellers, doctors, dentists, barbers, and photographers. In general, conditions improved slowly but steadily for the immigrants. By 1901, there were stricter laws governing the building of tenements. Functional bathrooms were now required in each apartment, rather than the earlier system of only two per floor.

There was fun as well in this new life. Children clutching their pennies made the candy store an informal social center. The delicatessen, serving a wealth of familiar foods, was also a draw. And soda fountains and dance halls offered places for teenagers to meet and flirt with each other. Best of all was a summer break from the city heat. Anyone who could afford to would leave the city for the nearby Catskill Mountains, where inexpensive boardinghouses provided green grass and fresh air. For those who could not afford even a short vacation, there was always the roof. On hot nights, whole families would sleep out on mattresses under the city lights and the pale stars.

Women sewing piecework at home

23

THE CHALLENGES OF A NEW WORLD

Orchard Street, Canal Street, Division Street—the streets of the Lower East Side were centers of bustling Jewish community life in the new world. Yet even though the Jews were used to living a hard life, their new home presented them with many difficulties.

To begin with, America in general and New York City specifically were very fast-paced. The hustle and bustle was totally new to people who had previously lived all their lives in quiet villages. Men who had been respected scholars now had to work as peddlers to make a living. Everything was different, and family and traditional religious life began to break down.

One of the most shocking symptoms of change was an increase in crime. Parents lost the old-fashioned authority they once had over their children, and kids began to get into trouble with the law. Jewish gangsters named Spanish Johnny, the Kid Dropper, Little Kisky, Gyp the Blood, and the notorious Louis Lepke struck fear into the hearts of law-abiding citizens.

Jewish family life continued to be strong in American cities, but change was everywhere. We take going to school for granted, but for Jewish kids, everything from the English language to American history made public school confusing.

A much-loved Jewish newspaper, the *Forward*, addressed the problems of the times. Its advice column, the "Bintel Brief," which means "bundle of letters," was full of tales of trouble: divorce, broken hearts, warring relatives, thankless children, and misunderstandings between the generations. The entire non-Jewish world was different from the Jewish immigrants' old life.

Rabbis, and religious beliefs in general, had less influence in New York than they had had in the Pale. But social work in part filled

Gangster Louis Lepke (right) being escorted by police

Jewish immigrants shared many things with other immigrants of the time, but Russian Jews were different in that many were skilled workers. A large majority made a living in some aspect of the clothing trade. About one-third of all immigrants eventually returned to their original countries, but a large percentage—nine-tenths—of Jewish immigrants stayed in the United States. In this they shared something with the Irish, who feared returning to their British landlords as much as the Jews feared living again under religious and political repression.

The streets of the Lower East Side were a child's playground

the role of religion. Lillian Wald (1867–1970) was a beloved figure on the street. She founded the Henry Street Settlement, which provided care and many important services to the immigrant community. Trained as a nurse, she dealt with everything from children bitten by rats to near-starvation resulting from poverty. Wald and her associates fought for parks, public nursing, and a limit to child labor. On the Lower East Side, a social worker was the closest thing to a saint.

Even Yiddish changed in the New World. Immigrants learned English to communicate with others, but most of them still spoke Yiddish at home. The combination of the two languages—"Yinkglish"—produced some amusing words: *alrightnik* referred to someone who has done well and boasts about it, and a bum was called a *no-goodnik*.

Often children adapted more easily to American ways than their parents and grandparents did. In fact, a proverb of the new country said, "In America, it is the children who raise the parents." Children learned English quickly, and were stimulated and excited by the city around them. As the older generation clung to the old ways, they often leaned on their children for help. This put strain on the structure of the family. But for all the disagreements, children and parents relied on each other, as did the entire Jewish community.

Social worker Lillian Wald

WESTWARD BOUND

Eastern European Jewish immigrants usually settled in New York City, but Jews from other European countries often headed west. Most of the first Jewish immigrants to reach American shores in the 1800s were from Germany, Austria, and Hungary. They made up the first large Jewish population in the United States. These German Jews, as they were called, spoke Yiddish and were religious people. A small number of them spread out over the entire continent, drawn west by the discovery of gold in California in 1848.

Before the Civil War, many German Jewish families lived alone on the frontier. This was a world without large grocery stores, department stores, or shopping malls.

Instead, frontier families relied on peddlers, traveling salesmen who carried a vast variety of goods. Many of the German Jews became peddlers of everything from tools and needles to toys and dress fabric.

Jewish peddlers and then merchants followed the railway lines. Soon there were Jewish communities in important transportation points such as Chicago, Milwaukee, and St. Louis. The United States was growing rapidly. In particular, the city of San Francisco was booming as a result of the gold rush. By the mid-1850s, there were 4,000 Jews living in this city on the bay. Jewish peddlers even followed prospectors into tiny communities in the Sierra Mountains, where they established themselves as shopkeepers.

American Jewish Archives

Frederick Knefler, A Union Army officer

During the Civil War, thousands of Jews served on the Union side. Jewish soldiers were killed or wounded at Bull Run and Gettysburg, Atlanta, and Shiloh. The highest-ranking Jewish officer in the Union Army was Brevet Brigadier-General Frederick Knefler. Company C of the 82nd Illinois Infantry was known as the Israelite Company, because most of its members were Jewish. Some southern Jews, however, joined with their neighbors to support the institution of slavery and states' rights. As soldiers, bandage rollers, and bond sellers, Jews served with their fellow Americans in many important roles during the Civil War.

A merchant peddles his wares

The German Jews had a fairly easy time becoming part of American life. They founded hospitals, synagogues, homes for the aged, and schools. Many groups gathered together to form the Young Men's Hebrew Association (YMHA), based on the Christian YMCA.

German Jews practiced Reform Judaism. This form of religion was modern: men no longer covered their heads while they prayed, men and women sat together in the synagogue, and dietary laws were not strictly observed. The German Jews had a tight-knit sense of community and relied on themselves, but they also loved America. By 1890, most of these immigrants were in business or were professionals. The German Jews had made it on their own terms as Americans.

Prospecting for California gold

PREJUDICE

The Jews from Europe faced more than the confusion of a new land when they entered the United States. They also faced prejudice. Some of this was the common prejudice directed against all immigrants, whether they were Jews, Italians, Greeks, or Poles. The flood of poor, foreign immigrants often frightened citizens of longer standing.

Anti-Semitism, discrimination against Jews, was unfortunately not new to America. After the Civil War, Jews were often portrayed in literature and the press as misers, one of the oldest and worst anti-Semitic stereotypes. Anti-Jewish feeling in America did not lead to the murder and destruction that it had in Russia and Poland. Instead, it led to social discrimination. By 1880, social clubs among the wealthy and powerful were excluding Jews. Summer resorts often advertised, "We prefer not to entertain Hebrews."

The appearance of religious Jews, who wore dark clothes, beards, and side curls called peyes *(PAY-ess)*, led to prejudice. Perhaps even worse was the American non-Jews' fear that the Russian Jews were radicals who brought bombs, union organizing, demonstrations, and revolution along with them from eastern Europe.

Discrimination took many forms. Laws were passed that restricted immigration. Prestigious universities often secretly limited the number of Jews they would admit. The same was true of medical and other professional schools.

Interestingly, it was not only the non-Jewish world that was prejudiced against the newcomers. Even Jews sometimes discriminated against other Jews. The German Jews had already established themselves in the United States. As a rule, they were middle-class and well integrated into American society. The German Jews felt threatened when the flood of Russian Jews arrived. The Russians were poorer, more foreign, and more radical than the Germans. German Jews wanted to limit immigration and often had their own country clubs and associations that would not admit Russian Jews.

Louis Brandeis, a Supreme Court justice fron 1916 to 1939

Was America really a melting pot? To this day, people of different cultural, religious, and racial backgrounds wonder how much of their identity they should give up to fit in. Some think differences are an important part of democracy; some want to blend in. Louis Brandeis (1856–1941), who was a United States Supreme Court justice and a supporter of Zionism, declared, "To be good Americans, we must be better Jews." Brandeis University in Waltham, Massachusetts, is named after this honorable man.

Tiles in the U.S. Holocaust Memorial Museum form a memorial to the 1.5 million Jewish children killed during the Holocaust

Still, most of the American Jews could not help but feel an interest in the new immigrants. After all, they shared a religion, a history, and common ideals of family and work. Often the German Jewish community helped the new immigrants, funding settlement houses and YMHAs, vocational and women's programs. In 1906, established members of the German Jewish community founded the American Jewish Committee, which was designed to meet the needs of the Jewish community in the United States.

The Jews of eastern Europe found that America was not perfect. Their lively and distinctive culture caused them to stand out from the American mainstream and made them the target of prejudice. In 1924, a U.S. government report referred to Jewish immigrants as a "ghetto type . . . filthy, un-American . . . twisted." But despite these problems, the new immigrants continued to rely on themselves and gradually established themselves as American citizens.

Jews were often barred from clubs and resorts

YIDDISH THEATER AND NEWSPAPERS

The Yiddish Theater was one of the most exciting things about life on New York's Lower East Side. The audience relaxed and enjoyed the show, taken away from their worries and hard lives by the singing, dancing, jokes, and tears of the theater. People particularly loved to see plays about family life and problems. If you went with your parents, you might very well fall asleep before the end of the play, since performances often went on past midnight. It was hard for many families to save even the few pennies needed for tickets, so they usually stayed late to get their money's worth.

The theater had plenty of clowns and comedians to take the audience's minds off their problems. Sometimes an actor might talk directly to the audience to complain about his relatives or even to invite the whole crowd to his wedding! If there was a problem backstage, an actor might simply be pushed in front of the curtain and have to entertain

The Bettmann Archive

Comedienne Fanny Brice takes a tumble

the audience until the play was ready to begin.

For the Jewish kids who hung out on the streets of New York, being an actor was a way out of poverty. Probably their mothers and fathers wanted them to be doctors or lawyers. But many children were inspired by the desire to crack jokes on the stage, to make a living singing and dancing. It certainly sounded like more fun than working hard all day in a sweatshop or even in an office. Many

Industrious boys went to work selling Yiddish newspapers on the street. They wore their dark caps pulled forward and had a hungry look in their eyes—hunger for a bigger life beyond the Lower East Side. Some of them dreamt about being writers or poets; even more of them dreamt about the traveling life of vaudeville, about the money to be made from singing and telling jokes.

An enterprising newspaper boy

The Marx Brothers—Chico (left), Groucho, and Harpo—clown around in the 1940 movie
Go West

of these children grew up to be entertainers whose names are still known today—Fanny Brice, Jack Benny, and Milton Berle, to name a few.

A young actor usually started in vaudeville, shows that traveled from town to town. Vaudeville had everything from comics to animal acts to serious entertainment, all on the same bill. The next step was to hit the big time, a large theater, and then shoot for that new invention, the movies.

The Marx Brothers were three stars who began their careers in vaudeville. They made many hilarious movies—including the slapstick classic *Duck Soup*—that are still shown in theaters today. Groucho twirled his mustache and wore funny glasses. Chico donned an odd hat and spoke in all kinds of accents. And Harpo never spoke but instead played the harp, tooted on a trumpet, and ate dozens of hard-boiled eggs without batting an eye.

The Lower East Side was a place where Yiddish culture could finally shine. Besides the theater, there were Yiddish newspapers that published all the gossip and news of the day. For example, the *Forward* was full of advice about how to cope with children. Many traditional fathers were ready to throw their smart-aleck kids out into the street—children who talked back, ran in gangs, and did not do what their parents told them to do. The newspaper's advice was always to keep the children at home in the hope that they would not go completely bad.

NEW FAMILIES

What was it like to be a Jewish kid growing up on the streets of New York? Parents worried about their children constantly. They were afraid that even an innocent game of stickball could lead to an accident, or worse, falling in with the wrong crowd and ending up in a gang. Parents sometimes even worried about school, because it was a foreign world.

In general, the kids loved school, and they wanted to learn. They wanted to become true Americans. Imagine what it would be like if your parents spoke a different language from English and seemed old-fashioned in their ideas and the way they dressed. Imagine if on the first day of school you could not understand a word the teacher said. Your clothes might be shabby or too big. Even your lunch might smell and look different from the other kids' lunches. Still, Jewish kids stayed in school, and many made it to City College, where they received the education they needed for a better life.

In the middle of the twentieth century, another change occurred for the Jewish community. As they became better educated and obtained better jobs, they began to consider leaving the streets of the Lower East Side. Mothers and fathers who had grown up playing "kick the can" and stickball on the stoop

The Jewish mother was the center of the immigrant family. She was even stronger in the new world than she had been in Europe because she held the family together. Some mothers raised their family alone, and most worked as seamstresses in addition to cooking, cleaning, and, of course, worrying about their wild American children.

A young boy asks the "Four Questions" on Passover

had a different dream for their children. They saw their kids playing in Little League on green fields in the suburbs, enjoying the opportunities of education and a rich life. If Grandma had come from Russia and had raised her daughter on the Lower East Side, it was likely that her grandchildren would be raised in the suburbs. There, each house sat separately on its own well-groomed lawn, and a station wagon was parked in nearly every driveway. It was a very different world from the noisy, bustling, colorful world of the Lower East Side.

Many older people chose to stay put in familiar places. If their grandchildren wanted to eat a really sour pickle, see men in dark hats and beards, buy some hot chestnuts from a pushcart, or hear Yiddish spoken, then they would go visit Grandma, who still kept her apartment on the Lower East Side.

The world of the immigrants was ending. Jews now lived in the suburbs of most of the major cities in the United States. This was the last stage of a long journey that had taken them from the dark times in Europe into a new way of life.

A suburban family visits Grandma and Grandpa in the city

NEW YORK CITY

New York is a teeming city, full of people from all over the world. To Jews, however, it is the Jewish capital of America. What makes New York America's most important Jewish city? Some people have a simple answer: delicatessens! You can go into a deli and order any kind of Jewish food from a hot pastrami sandwich on rye bread to cole slaw and Russian dressing—and don't forget the sour pickle!

The garment industry still flourishes along Eighth Avenue. You must walk carefully here and watch out for men pushing huge racks of everything from bulky coats to fancy dresses down the middle of the street. The diamond business is also an industry in which many Jewish families work. New York is also famous for its great orchestras and chamber music groups that play classical music nearly every night of the week. Famous Jewish musicians play violin and flute at the opera house and sometimes even in outdoor concerts in Central Park.

The Lower East Side was the neighborhood to which many Jewish immigrants flocked straight off the boat. It is still a lively neighborhood with a colorful street life. There, many big retail businesses are open on Sunday. Why? The original immigrants kept the Sabbath on Saturday, and Sunday shopping still remains a custom.

Traditional Hasids, who wear long black coats and fur hats, still live in communities in the New York borough of Brooklyn in areas called Williamsburg and Crown Heights.

In New York, there are signs of Jewish life everywhere. The Jewish Museum houses ancient gold and silver religious objects such as menorahs, which are candlesticks for the holiday of Hanukkah that hold nine candles. New York has many large Jewish hospitals, such as Mount Sinai and Beth Israel. It has even recently had two Jewish mayors, Abe Beam and Ed Koch.

A father treats his daughter to lunch at the dairy restaurant

When I was a little girl, my dad would take me to a Jewish dairy restaurant in New York to eat kasha varniskas. A dairy restaurant is kosher and does not serve meat. Kasha is buckwheat and tastes like nutty brown rice. It came in a big silver dish and was covered in hot gravy. Best of all, the varniskas were little noodles shaped like bow ties, hot and tasty. I remember that all the waiters wore bow ties, just the shape of the varniskas. They spoke Yiddish when they urged us to have seconds.

Traditional dress on Orchard Street, an established Jewish neighborhood in New York

Down at the tip of Manhattan Island, a borough of New York City, are three tiny cemeteries overgrown with plants. Here, a few headstones worn by age and soiled by air pollution still stand, engraved with the six-pointed Star of David, a Jewish symbol. These are the oldest Jewish cemeteries in the United States, surviving from when Spanish-speaking Jews came to the city that was then called New Amsterdam.

Don't forget the Statue of Liberty, which stands gleaming in New York harbor, still lifting her torch. Ellis Island is now a museum, a tribute to all the immigrants who dared to begin a new life in America.

Some say that the liveliness and energy of New York and its biting but good-natured sense of humor reflect the influence of Jewish culture. How about this New York Jewish joke? "If I had my life to live over again, I'd like to live it over a delicatessen." Would you? And don't forget to get a pastrami sandwich.

A kosher New York bakery

AMERICAN JEWS: FOUR LIVES

What did the Jews do in America? They threw themselves into the life of the country, excelling at everything from baseball to movie making. One of them even cured a deadly disease.

Sandy Koufax (b. 1935)

Take Sandy (Sanford) Koufax, for example. He was born in Brooklyn in 1935. He started off liking basketball better than baseball but instead became a famous pitcher and the youngest player to be chosen for the Baseball Hall of Fame. He was a great pitcher with four no-hit games for the Los Angeles Dodgers. A bad pitching hand forced him to retire when he was just 31 years old. Koufax won the hearts of his Jewish fans when he refused to play ball on Rosh Hashanah, the Jewish New Year, and still went on to help the Dodgers win the World Series.

Felix Frankfurter, defender of freedom of speech

Felix Frankfurter (1882–1965)

Felix Frankfurter was also a winner. He came to New York from Austria when he was only 12, without knowing any English. But he went on to serve as a judge on the U.S. Supreme Court, the highest court in the land. Throughout his career, he worked for peace. He was one of the founders of the American Civil Liberties Union, which helped lawyers defend such causes as freedom of speech. Even though he was a judge, Felix Frankfurter felt that the votes of the people themselves were more important than the decision of any court. Frankfurter believed that making mistakes, and learning from them, was part of democracy.

Sandy Koufax winds up to pitch

The gifted playwright, Lillian Hellman

Lillian Hellman (1905–1984)

Lillian Hellman believed in freedom of speech, too. She is considered to be one of the most important American playwrights. Her first play, *The Children's Hour* (1934), shows how a seemingly innocent child can ruin the lives of adults through some frighteningly evil behavior. Hellman's plays often looked at how lies and jealousy can destroy family life. She also wrote about the big picture—war and political events. In her later years, she wrote several books that looked back on people and places she had known, reflecting on the nature of how and what we remember. Two of these important works are *An Unfinished Woman* (1969) and *Pentimento* (1973).

Barbra Streisand (b. 1942)

Barbra Streisand was born *Barbara* in 1942. Changing the spelling of her name was just one small part of her creativity; she went on to become a renowned singer, movie actress, and film director and producer. Many of her records have sold more than a million copies. She first became a star while performing in *Funny Girl* on Broadway. In this musical comedy, Streisand portrayed Fanny Brice, who had also been a famous Jewish singer, dancer and comedienne. Raised poor in Brooklyn, Streisand knew she would be an actress by the time she was four years old. When she was starting out, she was told to change her last name to something that sounded less Jewish. Instead, she just changed her first name.

The glamorous star joined forces with Isaac B. Singer, the old Yiddish writer, to make a movie. Singer's story *Yentl* caught Barbra Streisand's attention. *Yentl* is the Yiddish story of a girl who passionately wants to study the Torah, the text of Jewish law. But girls are not allowed to study, so she disguises herself as a boy. Streisand directed and starred in this movie.

Barbra Streisand receiving a Grammy Award

JONAS SALK

Jonas Salk was a scientist who helped all of humanity. There was once a deadly disease that attacked mostly children and young people. Every summer this plague swept through America and left thousands of children paralyzed for life. Some lost the use of their arms or legs, and many died. Mothers and fathers worried about this terror. Sometimes they would not let their children go swimming, because the disease could be caught in a pool. Sometimes they took their kids to the country, hoping they could escape the disease by escaping from the city. But there was no escape, and no cure.

This disease was called polio (poliomyelitis). The scientist who fought this disease and won was Jonas Salk. He invented the anti-polio vaccine that eliminated polio throughout the United States.

Jonas Salk was born in 1914 in Upper Manhattan. Like many Jewish New Yorkers, his father worked in the garment district, manufacturing clothing. When the family moved, he went to grade school in the Bronx. He read constantly and tried to be perfect in his schoolwork and get the highest grades. He went on to become a doctor and worked

Dr. Salk often worked 16 hours a day, six days a week, only taking off Sundays to be with his three sons. Not only did he work tirelessly to develop a vaccine against polio, he also taught at the universities of Michigan and Pittsburgh. From 1963 to 1975, he was the director of the Salk Institute for Biological Studies at the University of California, San Diego. Today, at age 79, he and his colleagues at the Salk Institute are working to develop a vaccine against AIDS, a deadly disease of the immune system.

Jonas Salk in 1955, working to perfect his polio vaccine

in New York's large Jewish hospital, Mount Sinai.

In about 1947, at the University of Pittsburgh, Dr. Salk became fascinated with the virus that causes polio. He began to hunt it. He soon discovered that there were actually three kinds of virus that caused the disease. A vaccine would have to fight all three. In 1953, Dr. Salk tested his new polio vaccine on one hundred kids and adults. None of them got sick or died. But the year before, 3,300 people had died in the polio epidemic. Dr. Salk had to move fast to prevent another disaster.

With the consent of their parents, first 5,000 children and then one million received the polio vaccine. Many were afraid of the needle, but their parents knew the shot might someday save their lives. Soon, almost every child in America was routinely given a polio vaccine. Today, there is no more polio in the United States.

Before the Salk vaccine, summer could be a time of dread. Would polio strike your family? Would you end up unable ever to walk again? Would your brother's arm become small and weak? Would your sister need many operations on her spine? When you went back to school in September, would you learn that some of your classmates had died from polio? Dr. Salk is a hero to the world's children because he made their lives safe from a terrible disease.

THE JEWS' INFLUENCE ON AMERICA

If you see a bigger kid hitting a smaller one, what is your reaction? Some people are not bothered by a bully's strength; others always root for the underdog. The Jews had been underdogs in Europe and had to struggle to survive in the United States. These experiences led them to take the side of the underdog. Social justice for everyone has always been an important Jewish ideal.

Many immigrants started their new life by working in sweatshops manufacturing clothing. It was hard work, badly paid, with long hours. These workers knew they were being taken advantage of. They began to band together to form labor unions. Unions such as the International Ladies' Garment Workers made sure that its workers were paid a fair wage and did not have to work in unsafe buildings. Jewish workers were active throughout American unions and brought their ideal of social justice to the labor movement.

American Jewish Archives

Albert Einstein, world-famous physicist who also worked for peace

Americans from all walks of life enjoy Jewish foods

A few years ago, posters appeared in the subway in New York City saying, "You Don't Have To Be Jewish To Eat Levy's Rye Bread." The pictures showed Chinese grandfathers, black school kids, and all-American cheerleaders biting into delicious deli sandwiches. In America, you don't have to be Jewish to eat bagels with cream cheese or a kosher hot dog with sauerkraut. Jewish food, like the Jewish immigrants, have become a part of all of our lives.

Jews have entered and excelled in many professions

The National Association for the Advancement of Colored People, or the NAACP, was not an organization based on helping the Jews. It was formed in 1910 to protect the rights of African Americans. But Jews, because they knew what it was like to suffer from prejudice, became active in the organization. In fact, the NAACP has had two Jewish presidents. Jewish lawyers, including Felix Frankfurter, who later became a Supreme Court justice, often fought for equal rights for everyone.

On a lighter note, think of something that is a favorite pastime for many of us— going to the movies. Many Jews who had entertained on stage, such as vaudeville actors, moved to Hollywood when movies first started to be made. As a result, many of the top studio executives of Paramount, Metro-Goldwyn-Mayer, Warner Brothers, and United Artists came from immigrant Jewish families. They seemed to have a knack for knowing what the public loved—westerns, romantic close-ups, war dramas, action, and

adventure. Comedy, in particular, was influenced by the jokes and routines of Jewish vaudeville. Next time you hear someone on television use the old joke, "Take my mother-in-law . . . please!" or "That was no lady; that was my wife," you will know an old joke— some would say too old!—from Jewish vaudeville.

The Jews who came to America had big dreams. They dreamed of a country where it was safe to work and raise a family. Their dreams led them to work for social justice for everyone, not just for Jews. Jews have become successful and made important contributions in all professions. Their dreams were also creative and artistic. In the old country, there was not much time for entertainment or art. In America, Jews became writers, novelists, and poets. They became painters and sculptors, they created movies and television. They became rock 'n' roll singers and famous violinists. America made it possible for their dreams to grow, and they gave America their dreams.

JEWISH LIFE TODAY

What is life like for most Jews today in the United States? If you are Jewish, you probably do not wear a yarmulke or peyes if you are a boy. You do not wear a kerchief over your braids if you are a girl. If you play the violin, you probably also play baseball, and your life may be much like that of your non-Jewish friends and neighbors.

Still, you probably value education as much as your immigrant grandparents or great-grandparents did. And you feel strong ties to your family and to your heritage. Two things happened in the last fifty years to influence how American Jews feel. The first of these was the Nazi Holocaust (1933–1945) in Europe in which six million Jews were killed.

The Jewish culture of the shtetl, the original home of so many Jews who came to America, was destroyed.

The second event that greatly influenced American Jews was the formation in 1948 of the state of Israel as a Jewish homeland. The formation of Israel led to another wave of Jewish immigration, as Jews from the United States, the former Soviet Union (Russia), and other countries returned to the land that had been their people's home more than 2,000 years earlier. In fact, about half of the four million Jews in Israel are immigrants or the children of immigrants.

Although American Jews were geographically far from both the Holocaust and the formation of Israel, they consider these

James Mairs

Most American Jews live in New York City

The United States Holocaust Memorial Museum opened in 1993

events to be part of the history that all Jews share. For many American Jews, World War II (1939–1945) was a reminder always to remember and understand their own history. Even though many lived comfortable lives rich in education, family, and freedom, American Jews knew they should never forget the more difficult parts of their history.

If you are Jewish, you probably have your own ways of remembering your history. Perhaps you have a special Hebrew name that might be your regular name or one you use only on religious occasions. Perhaps you have visited Israel and explored the ancient city of Jerusalem or helped Israeli Jews harvest oranges on a *kibbutz* (a farming cooperative). In the United States, the recent opening of the Holocaust Memorial Museum in Washington, D.C., is part of a national pledge to remember—and avoid repeating—the past. Ellis Island is now a museum that exhibits old photographs and offers a guided tour. The

names of immigrants are printed on the tiles of the museum wall to honor these early Americans for their courage. These tiles were donated by the children and grandchildren of American immigrants.

Jews throughout history have endured many trials and achieved many victories. Despite these changes and upheavals in Jewish life, American Jews still love to celebrate traditional holidays. Take Passover, for example, the major Jewish holiday. It occurs in the spring and celebrates how the Jews escaped from slavery in Egypt in ancient times. On Passover, Jewish families travel to be together for a feast called a seder. Certain foods eaten during seder tell a story. Dipping celery in salt water, for example, represents the tears the Jews shed in slavery. The youngest child in the family has a special role during seder. He or she gets to ask the four questions about Passover, starting with, "Why is this night different from every other night?"

In the Old World, Hanukkah was a simple winter holiday that celebrated a long-ago uprising against a cruel leader. The holiday was marked by the lighting of candles in a menorah over eight days. This symbolized the Hanukkah story, in which a small vial of oil in the Jewish temple burned miraculously for eight days. In Russia, Hanukkah was celebrated by eating potato pancakes fried in golden oil. But like so many aspects of Jewish life, Hanukkah changed when it came to America. Some families exchange gifts on Hanukkah, which falls near Christmas. In fact, some children get one present on each of the eight nights of Hanukkah.

Many American Jewish children celebrate a bar mitzvah (for boys) or a bat mitzvah (for girls). This event marks a child's thirteenth birthday. He or she stands before the congregation in the synagogue and recites a passage in Hebrew or gives a speech. Afterward, there is a big party. This ceremony shows that a person is becoming an adult. In the midst of the modern world, these old traditions still hold beauty and meaning.

Three generations come together to celebrate Hanukkah

Jewish life in America is a blend of the old and the new

Jewish life today is a blend of the old and the new. History is very important to the Jewish community, but so is the future. On the mantelpiece in a typical Jewish home, for example, you might find faded black-and-white photographs from the Old Country. One might be of a man with a beard and a woman with her hair in a bun. These are the great-grandparents, who came from Russia to the Lower East Side. Next to them are photos of their son in his World War II uniform and their daughter in a college cap and gown. Then there are photos of the grandchildren, dressed in bellbottoms, with long hair, backpacks, and big smiles. And finally there is a photo of a new baby, the third generation to be born in America, looking into the twenty-first century.

INDEX

Other books about Jewish Americans and immigration:

Nonfiction
Finkelstein, Norman. *The Other 1492: Jewish Settlement in the New World.* New York: William Morrow, 1992.

Levine, Ellen. *If Your Name Was Changed at Ellis Island.* Scholastic, Inc., 1992.

Metzer, Milton. *The Jews in America: A Picture Album.* Philadelphia: Jewish Publication Society, 1985.

Rosenblum, Richard. *Journey to the Golden Land.* Philadelphia: Jewish Publication Society, 1992.

Fiction
Lasky, Kathryn. *The Night Journey.* New York: Puffin, 1986.

Levitin, Sonia. *Journey to America.* New York: MacMillan, 1987.

Singer, Isaac Bashevis. *Naftali: The Storyteller and His Horse* and *A Tale of Three Wishes.* New York: Farrar, Strauss & Giroux, 1976.

BIZARRE & BEAUTIFUL SERIES

A spirited and fun investigation of the mysteries of the five senses in the animal kingdom.

Each title is 8¹/₂″ x 11″, 48 pages, $14.95 hardcover, with color photographs and illustrations throughout.

Bizarre & Beautiful Ears
Bizarre & Beautiful Eyes
Bizarre & Beautiful Feelers
Bizarre & Beautiful Noses
Bizarre & Beautiful Tongues

RAINBOW WARRIOR ARTISTS SERIES

What is a Rainbow Warrior Artist? It is a person who strives to live in harmony with the Earth and all living creatures, and who tries to better the world while living his or her life in a creative way.

Each title is written by Reavis Moore with a foreword by LeVar Burton, and is 8¹/₂″ x 11″, 48 pages, $14.95 hardcover, with color photographs and illustrations.

Native Artists of Africa (available 1/94)
Native Artists of North America

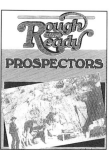
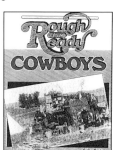

ROUGH AND READY SERIES

Learn about the men and women who settled the American frontier. Explore the myths and legends about these courageous individuals and learn about the environmental, cultural, and economic legacies they left to us.

Each title is written by A. S. Gintzler and is 48 pages, 8¹/₂″ x 11″, $12.95 hardcover, with two-color illustrations and duotone archival photographs.

Rough and Ready Cowboys (available 4/94)
Rough and Ready Homesteaders (available 4/94)
Rough and Ready Prospectors (available 4/94)

AMERICAN ORIGINS SERIES

Many of us are the third and fourth generation of our families to live in America. Learn what our great-great grandparents experienced when they arrived here and how much of our lives are still intertwined with theirs.

Each title is 48 pages, 8¹/₂″ x 11″, $12.95 hardcover, with two-color illustrations and duotone archival photographs.

Tracing Our German Roots, Leda Silver
Tracing Our Irish Roots, Sharon Moscinski
Tracing Our Italian Roots, Kathleen Lee
Tracing Our Jewish Roots, Miriam Sagan

ORDERING INFORMATION
Please check your local bookstore for our books, or call 1-800-888-7504 to order direct from us. All orders are shipped via UPS; see chart to calculate your shipping charge for U.S. destinations. **No P.O. Boxes please; we must have a street address to ensure delivery.** If the book you request is not available, we will hold your check until we can ship it. Foreign orders will be shipped surface rate unless otherwise requested; please enclose $3.00 for the first item and $1.00 for each additional item.

METHODS OF PAYMENT
Check, money order, American Express, MasterCard, or Visa. We cannot be responsible for cash sent through the mail. For credit card orders, include your card number, expiration date, and your signature, or call (800) 888-7504. American Express card orders can be shipped only to billing address of cardholder. Sorry, no C.O.D.'s. Residents of sunny New Mexico, add 6.125% tax to total.

Address all orders and inquiries to:
John Muir Publications
P.O. Box 613
Santa Fe, NM 87504
(505) 982-4078
(800) 888-7504

For U.S. Orders Totaling	Add
Up to $15.00	$4.25
$15.01 to $45.00	$5.25
$45.01 to $75.00	$6.25
$75.01 or more	$7.25

EXTREMELY WEIRD SERIES

All of the titles are written by Sarah Lovett, 8½" x 11", 48 pages, $9.95 paperbacks, with color photographs and illustrations.

Extremely Weird Bats
Extremely Weird Birds
Extremely Weird Endangered Species
Extremely Weird Fishes
Extremely Weird Frogs
Extremely Weird Insects
Extremely Weird Mammals
Extremely Weird Micro Monsters
Extremely Weird Primates
Extremely Weird Reptiles
Extremely Weird Sea Creatures
Extremely Weird Snakes
Extremely Weird Spiders

X-RAY VISION SERIES

Each title in the series is 8½" x 11", 48 pages, $9.95 paperback, with color photographs and illustrations and written by Ron Schultz.

Looking Inside the Brain
Looking Inside Cartoon Animation
Looking Inside Caves and Caverns
Looking Inside Sports Aerodynamics
Looking Inside Sunken Treasure
Looking Inside Telescopes and the Night Sky

THE KIDDING AROUND TRAVEL GUIDES

All of the titles listed below are 64 pages and $9.95 paperbacks, except for *Kidding Around the National Parks* and *Kidding Around Spain*, which are 108 pages and $12.95 paperbacks.

Kidding Around Atlanta
Kidding Around Boston, 2nd ed.
Kidding Around Chicago, 2nd ed.
Kidding Around the Hawaiian Islands
Kidding Around London
Kidding Around Los Angeles
Kidding Around the National Parks
  of the Southwest
Kidding Around New York City, 2nd ed.
Kidding Around Paris
Kidding Around Philadelphia
Kidding Around San Diego
Kidding Around San Francisco
Kidding Around Santa Fe
Kidding Around Seattle
Kidding Around Spain
Kidding Around Washington, D.C., 2nd ed.

MASTERS OF MOTION SERIES

Each title in the series is 10¼" x 9", 48 pages, $9.95 paperback, with color photographs and illustrations.

How to Drive an Indy Race Car
  David Rubel
How to Fly a 747
  Tim Paulson
How to Fly the Space Shuttle
  Russell Shorto

THE KIDS EXPLORE SERIES

Each title is written by kids for kids by the Westridge Young Writers Workshop, 7" x 9", with photographs and illustrations by the kids.

Kids Explore America's Hispanic Heritage
112 pages, $7.95 paper
Kids Explore America's African-American Heritage
128 pages, $8.95 paper
Kids Explore the Gifts of Children with Special Needs
112 pages, $8.95 paper (available 2/94)
Kids Explore America's Japanese Heritage
112 pages, $8.95 paper (available 4/94)

ENVIRONMENTAL TITLES

Habitats: Where the Wild Things Live
Randi Hacker and Jackie Kaufman
8½" x 11", 48 pages, color illustrations, $9.95 paper

The Indian Way: Learning to Communicate with Mother Earth
Gary McLain
7" x 9", 114 pages, illustrations, $9.95 paper

Rads, Ergs, and Cheeseburgers:
The Kids' Guide to Energy and the Environment
Bill Yanda
7" x 9", 108 pages, two-color illustrations, $13.95 paper

The Kids' Environment Book:
What's Awry and Why
Anne Pedersen
7" x 9", 192 pages, two-color illustrations, $13.95 paper

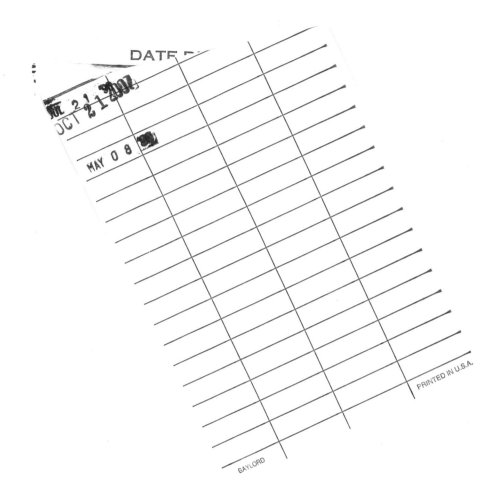

DATE D

OCT 21

MAY 0 8

PRINTED IN U.S.A.

GAYLORD